GRE🗺T

BY

THOMAS ALEXANDER

An Allegory In Four Acts

A REMOTE ROOM IN THE THROES OF WINTER.

THE ONCE GREAT MAN LIVES ALONE NOW WITH HIS SON,

AN OLD FRIEND HAS COME TO VISIT.

HE HAS CLIMBED UP FROM THE VILLAGE IN ORDER TO OFFER THE OLD MAN ONE LAST CHANCE TO ESCAPE THE ENCROACHING WINTER THAT IS ABOUT TO TAKE HIM, STIRRING UP MEMORIES OF BETTER TIMES AND THE WARMTH OF SUMMER.

Great by Thomas Alexander

Direct Light Publications
45 Dudley Court, Endell Street, London, WC2H 9RF

For Worldwide Performance Rights please contact Thomas Alexander at Direct Light Productions
thomasalexander@directlight-publications.com

Permissions may be sought directly from:
Publishing Rights Department, 45 Dudley Court, Endell Street, London, WC2H 9RF
Email: info@directlight-publications.com
Library of Congress Cataloguing in Publication Data
Application submitted.
British Library Cataloguing in Publication Data
Application submitted.
04 05 06 07 08 09 10 9 8 7 6 5 4 3 2
uuid:6452fce2-cd8b-440b-8205-8a7a1a32ea04
ISBN: 978-1-941979-02-0

–

Edited by Shirin Laghai for Direct Light Publications.

Available in Ebook and Soft Cover from Direct Light
Ebook ISBN: 978-1-941979-03-7

Cover design by SimplyA© 2014
simplya@directlight-publications.com

For London
Which I love more than is reasonable.
And which gave me the world.

GREAT

BY

THOMAS ALEXANDER

ABOUT THE AUTHOR

Thomas Alexander has worked in almost all forms of theatre, from opera to children's performances, working as everything from stage hand to costume designer, and has seen his work translated into four different languages and performed as far afield as America and Afghanistan.

His plays; *Writing William, Begat, Great, The Visitor* & *Murder Me Gently* along with his novel; *A Scattering Of Orphans* have been published by DIRECT LIGHT.

Also by the Author

PLAYS

Happiness
Murder Me Gently
The Family
Begat
The Crossroads Country
Great
The Visitor
When Dusk Brings Glory
The Recruitment Officer
Writer's Block
The Last Christmas
Writing William
The Big Match

NOVELS

A Scattering Of Orphans

ONE ACT PLAYS

Four Widows and A Funeral
For Arts Sake
The TV
Life TM
The Dance

ADAPTATIONS

William Shakespeare's' R3
Othello

GREAT

THOMAS ALEXANDER

Acknowledgements

My thanks go out to the State Library of Victoria in Melbourne where I first conceived the idea for Great and completed the first draft.

The original draft was written on a Blackberry Playbook in August 2012 and subsequently updated in London over the next two years.

As always my many thanks go out to the friends and industry professionals who gave valued input and direction.

FORWARD

by Thomas Alexander

The rise and counter-rise of nationalism in the past decade has been well documented and often talked about. The impact of globalisation and a migratory workforce, coupled with the increase of terrorism in the west and the cultural combat of new media, has led to a large sense of disenfranchisement with the forces of multiculturalism.

From the referendum over Scottish independence (which, at time of writing, is still to take place) to the moves to create a Sunni caliphate by ISIS, nationalism is clearly a growing part of the world we live in, if not the final dividing factor.

Whether it's Ukrainian inclusion in the EU, Russia's annexation of the Crimean Peninsula, the Arab Spring movement, or the rise of the Tea Party, nothing has become as contentious or important as nationalism. Who we are as a nation and who we are not. Who we wish to be and who we wish to be seen as. These are all under attack, and the attack comes not from the outside, but from within. Within our own borders. Within our own streets. Within our own selves.

When I was a youth I saw a comedian construct this argument perfectly, and his outline of the calibrations of nationalism remains the strongest I have seen. I don't remember the comedians name; he wasn't particularly famous, nor, I suppose, did his show do incredibly well as he dropped off the face of the earth and, despite numerous attempts over the years, I can find no trace of him. Nevertheless, the argument ran thus;

I am British,

Not the north. Not the north, but the south. The south!

Not the real south, but London. London!

Not North London, but South London. South London!

Not the very south, but Clapham. Clapham!

Not the centre, but my parents' house. My parents' house!

Not their room, but my room. My room!

I am my room!

And this, he concluded, was how nationalism worked, dividing again and again like Matryoshka dolls until we were sure that only people like us still existed.

C.S. Lewis said that we read to know we are not alone. That maybe true, but as Douglas Adams pointed out sometimes we find that we are not alone by discovering other cultures we never knew existed and are filled with the joyous wish to destroy them.

This, it seems, is the curse of understanding and it is a self-perpetuating problem that has no end. The rise of the Mujahidin in Afghanistan was in response to the Soviet occupation of the 1980s. The rise of the Taliban was in response to their excesses in victory. The rise of Al Qaeda was a response to western encroachment in the Middle East, and ISIS a response to their failure to enact lasting change.

With each permutation, stagnation leads to mutation. Whatever is the norm is questioned. It is one thing to support a brother-in-arms, but yet another to agree on how far his tree should encroach into your yard once you've laid down your guns. One man's prayer is another man's sacrilege. One man's justice, another's crime. Any nation that looks to define itself by fear and exclusion is one that is doomed to self-destruction, as north turns on south and a child's bedroom against a parent's.

In the weeks preceding the writing of this introduction, Prime Minister David Cameron declared that Britain needed to look to "British values" in response to an increase in Islamic teachings in schools. That the so-called values he referenced are intrinsic human rights, largely drawn out in the UN declaration of 1945, had no bearing, nor the fact that values such as fairness, justice, and freedom were counter-pinned by public surveillance, gagging orders, secret trials and governmental financial abuses.

Britain is not the first country to attempt to redefine itself in this way. France and, to a lesser extent, the United States of America have tried similar tacks in the face of neo-nationalism, attempting definitions to reunite a fractured community that has long since done away with the notion of country. And it is highly unlikely that "British values" will unite any better than the Gettysburg Address.

And herein lies the problem. Countries have long since become antiquated concepts, second to and guided, if not controlled outright, by multinationals who have no dependence on nations save their acquiescence, but who alter the lives of the people more rapidly and more forcefully than any government ever could. For a government – for a nationality – to remain relevant in the modern age, it must provide something for its citizens that a corporation cannot. Yet as free markets increasingly remove the possibility of a true middle class and shift the gap between rich and poor to unheard of heights, there seems little a country can offer its people outside of a passport and easy entry visas, so that this control is increasingly identified in the form of nationalism, racism, neocolonialism, and religion.

We read to know we are not alone. And if we cannot find ourselves in the lives of others, then we will find something with which to mould them to, or exclude them from. Be it the Bible. Be it the colour of our skin. Be it our taste in food, the clothes we wear, the music we listen to, or – to coin a talented comedian – the wallpaper in our parent's bedroom.

Luckily this has very little to do with the play. An allegory is just that, and what it means, what it is saying about Britain, is very much up to the reader to interpret.

The play was written in Australia in 2012 and edited over the next two years. I owe, as always, its completion to my wife, Shirin Laghai, without whom it would be nothing but an analogy in a writer's brain. Gethin's story about taxing words is all hers, and I am grateful to her for letting me use it as my own.

Thomas Alexander - London 2014

GREAT

Old England Is Dying

The Waterboys; Old England
(Composer: Mike Scott)

Great

An Allegory in 4 Acts

Cast

CONSTANTINE - An old man.

REMUS - A middle aged man. A foreigner.

GETHIN - A young man/teenager. Son to CONSTANTINE.

AMERICA - A young woman/teenager. Wife to CONSTANTINE.

ACT 1

ACT 1

Out on the far coast of nowhere, the wind lives caught and cut, rattling and moaning everything in its wake. Snowflakes on every breeze. Breathe in fog binders. Colder than cold.

A house, poor and sparse, wood and dust holding it up.

Two rough beds, no more than sacks, lie on either side of the room. Between them a table with two chairs, poor and well-worn, sit, sturdy and unmoving. A bottle and a cleaving knife are centre.

An old wood burning stove lies at the back of the room next to the door, a skillet on top used for cooking, a rough pot sitting central.

Two windows near the door show what appears to be a snow storm outside. Wind buffets the room and the entire theatre. It is cold. Snow seeps in through cracks in the door and windows, neither of which are closed properly, and swirls around the stage.

The room is timeless in that it could exist at any period in the 10th to 20th centuries, but there is no semblance of modern technology.

Time passes.

More time passes.

The door bursts open, whipping snow and wind across the stage. An old man, CONSTANTINE, struggles in through the storm. He is covered in a blanket to protect him, his clothes holed and threadbare.

In his gloved hand he holds a brace of rabbits caught in one of his snares.

The carcasses are frozen.

He is having trouble closing the door against the snow. He leans his frail frame against it, but has to drop the rabbits before he has the leverage to finally get it closed.

Snow has crept deep into the house and the old man eyes it as he picks up the rabbits. There is not enough heat in the cabin to melt the snow and so, placing the rabbits on the table, he uses a brush to gather the drift before bending with difficulty to shovel it off the floor and into the stove.

He collects wood from the corner of the room

and stacks it into the stove before going to a shelf, taking a book and tearing pages out. He delicately places them into the stove, careful so that the wind doesn't drag them away.

He digs a box of ageless matches out from inside his shirt. The wind tries to stop them lighting, but his practiced fingers get it at the first go, and he lights the papers and drops them into the stove.

A thin light waves from the stove and he warms his hands over it.

CONSTANTINE goes to the table, takes the stiff rabbits, and puts them next to the warmth.

There is a loud knock at the door.

The old man goes over to the window and looks out. He turns, shuffles to the door, and pulls it open as little as possible.

Two figures enter.

GETHIN, the old man's son, is as ragged and threadbare as he is. A virtual child, no more than a stick figure. With him is REMUS, old but not as old as CONSTANTINE, and considerably better dressed.

They both enter quickly, eager to escape the

cold, but though REMUS is keen to shake the snow and cold from his clothes, GETHIN remains obstinate, going quickly to a corner away from the other men and curling into it. Feral. Watching.

Together REMUS and CONSTANTINE manage to get the door closed again. CONSTANTINE moves wordlessly to the table and the bottle.

REMUS watches the old man, pity and revulsion in equal measures. He thinks about removing his gloves but realizing that the cold inside is almost as bad as outside he stops, casting instead a sad eye around the cabin.

This was the heart of his youth. A place of love and warmth. Now it is a decayed memory, much like CONSTANTINE.

REMUS   Can't keep doing this, Constantine.

CONSTANTINE wordlessly pulls out a chair for REMUS to sit on. He glares at GETHIN who holds his look.

REMUS sits.

CONSTANTINE takes two glasses and rubs

them clean on his rags.

CONSTANTINE   Where?

REMUS   Timian's. Market.

CONSTANTINE scoops up fallen snow into
the glasses and puts them on the table before
pouring two drinks.

CONSTANTINE   He's an idiot.

REMUS watches him closely, shocked at what
he's seeing. CONSTANTINE clinks glasses and
sits. REMUS thinks about the statement, and
puts the glass to one side before replying.

REMUS   Maybe. Yes. This can't go
on, Constantine.

CONSTANTINE drinks. Sipping, savouring.
The first in a long time. A special occasion.

CONSTANTINE   He'll be hurt. You have my
word.

REMUS thinks about this, then picks up his
glass and downs it in one, disgusted by the
comment as much as the drink.

CONSTANTINE is angered by his rush and
doesn't offer to pour another.

REMUS   You remember Narvid? Of

course you remember Narvid. He was... He was Narvid. (PAUSE) We expected you there, Constantine. (PAUSE) I can't keep vouching for the boy.

CONSTANTINE   Had to hunt.

REMUS looks around. Spies the frozen rabbits.

REMUS   He was at your wedding. (LONG PAUSE) You're not even going to ask what he stole?

CONSTANTINE looks at him, then uncorks the bottle and pours again. No snow. It sits untouched by REMUS.

REMUS (cont.)   It was his horse, you remember? At the wedding? Eighteen hands at least. All I heard, outside the church, stamp, stamp. You remember?

CONSTANTINE stares out of the window, wishing the man to leave.

CONSTANTINE   Storm's coming.

REMUS turns to look.

REMUS   Doesn't matter. The boy... He loved you, you know? Narvid. Her too, but you. That horse... You remember? Lost it at the end. Nothing you can do about that, I think. We all lose it at the end. Mind and body, eh?

CONSTANTINE   You burn him?

REMUS nods and drinks.

REMUS   Ground's too hard.

CONSTANTINE nods.

REMUS (cont.)   We thought you'd come.

CONSTANTINE   He'll work. The boy. For Timian.

REMUS   (AMUSED) Gethin? Work. Yes. Pocket's full, no doubt. Give him a week, he'll have the store. I'll… I'll pass it on to Timian. He'll be thrilled.

He drinks again, nearly choking. Then, without asking, refills.

CONSTANTINE notes the knife on the table.

REMUS (cont.)   It doesn't matter. This is what I came to tell you. Narvid… You didn't even ask how he died.

CONSTANTINE   No.

REMUS   Found him four feet from his door. Four feet. Stooped on the step. Drifting…. Thawing… (PAUSE) Won't see a fire like that in some time.

CONSTANTINE   Say it.

REMUS looks at him and thinks. He is not in a hurry.

REMUS   I caught this fish, before the storm hit. The lake… (BEAT) When was the last time you ate fish, Constantine? What do you… There's a hole. On the far side, no one else knows about it. Only me. It's where – do you remember – it's where we used to dive. In the summers. Same place. It's shaded and the ice doesn't get too thick and you can hole it with your boot if you know it well enough. And, well, I did. Hole it. And… It was a good day, you remember? Good sun on your neck. Not looking to catch anything, just… fishing. Not looking to catch anything. And… Third hour, nothing but the sun and the branches, you know what I mean? Beautiful. And I feel it. You know? A pull. Nothing big, just the gentlest of pulls, like he's slowly leaning against it, you know what I mean? So… I ease, nothing much. Ease. And snap! Just like that! Now, I'm running the line, everything I've got to keep the reel in my hand, you know what I mean? Twenty, thirty! And I'm thinking, how much line do I have, and snap! My arms! Nearly out their sockets! So, I'm hauling. This is not a good line. I'm not looking to catch anything, you understand? But I'm hauling all the same. And I can feel it, you know? The sun on my neck. Hours are passing. Reel. Release. But now all I'm thinking about is how I don't want to lose the rod, you know? Can't reach for my knife! I take a hand off the rod, it's gone. Far too big for the line. So, no choice. Reel and release. Who gets tired first, you know? And... I'm calling. To the fish, I'm calling! Talking to him. Why you want my rod? You think this is going to do you any good? Rod like this one hanging out your mouth? How you going to eat with a rod like this behind you? Who'll want you? And I can feel it, you know? Going down on my neck. The sun. Fingers... like ice! But what can I do? I've got a home, I tell him. A woman is waiting for me! I promise everything. Let him go. Everything. And I can see them, you know, the shadows, getting the light.

(RESIGNED) Anyway. (BANGING THE TABLE) Boom! He hits the ice, right beneath my feet! And I can feel him. The size on him! Turned on me! Boom, right under me! All I can do to hang on.

And the hole. It's closing. I can see it. Closing around the line. Can he even take the rod? And I guess he's thinking the same thing because this time, this time, he comes for me through the hole!

Now, it's dark. Shadows only and… Is it his nose, his head? I can't tell, but I've got him. Tight. Two feet of line maximum! Right in the palm of my hand, and I'm thinking, who cares about the cold! Who cares about dinner! This! This is dinner! Twenty dinners! War! You know what I mean? I've got him. Water, ice – red!

He sits back. Resigned.

REMUS (cont.)　　Can't get the hole big enough. Can't do it! Touched it. Right there. Twenty… Can't do it. (BEAT) Watched the line sink right into the ice. Rod with it. (PAUSE) Couldn't even free him.

He drinks and pours again, not caring about the glass any more. CONSTANTINE watches again, angry.

CONSTANTINE   You're leaving.

REMUS   (BITTER AT THE DRINK)
We're leaving. The Village. All of us. (PAUSE)
Two days. Three, if the weather holds up. This
is no place for a man, Constantine. No matter
the history.

CONSTANTINE rises. He heads to the stove,
glaring at GETHIN.

A sense of violence pervades the room.

Silence

CONSTANTINE   Stay for rabbit.

REMUS   No. (PAUSE) It's decided.
Three days at the latest, Constantine.

Pause.

CONSTANTINE   Storms won't last.

Pause.

REMUS   It's decided.

Pause.

CONSTANTINE   (ENDING THE CONVER-
SATION) Tell Timian he'll be hurt.

REMUS   And that's that?

Pause.

CONSTANTINE   Yes.

REMUS drinks again, choking. He looks set to leave but suddenly decided against it and pours himself another.

REMUS   No. No. Come. Sit down, Constantine. Sit down! I'll pay you for another bottle. Sit down!

CONSTANTINE sits, the knife close to him on the table. It is a gesture not unnoticed by REMUS, but his mind is set.

REMUS (cont.)   There's no lightning here! You know that. Not anymore. When we were young… (PAUSE) We're going across the lake. All of us. Far ridge. There has to be… (PAUSE) The boy doesn't deserve this.

CONSTANTINE   You pay for the whole bottle.

Silence. GETHIN stirs. REMUS pours.

REMUS   There is this man. He comes into the camp from time to time. Not from here. He brings goods, things to sell. Lightning. He comes, maybe a month ago. A little more. He brings with him this… box. A lightening box, he says. So, I say to him. What is that to me?

This is not a large box, maybe the size of your head. Little bigger. So, he says to me, he says, this box is the future. I swear! This box is the future! Just like that. He tells me everyone can get this box. Everyone! Where he comes from this is normal. So obviously I believe none of it. OK, I say, the future. Sure. But he is buying the bottle so I listen. This box, he says, this box everybody has. And this box... This is all you need, yes? Simple as that. With this box you can... Snow does not come in the door like that! Snow inside, this is a thing of the past. Rabbits... Whatever you want! So I say, sure, sure! Completely. And then he shows me! So simple! So... Like nothing you have ever seen. Just a box! And standing there, like that! He says to me, stand up, so... Like that. And he opens the box. And there, there, right there! Every detail! A picture of me. Like that! No time, no.... (HE FUMBLES FOR THE WORD) sulphur... Phosphorous. No phosphorous! Nothing. Like that. Just there! He takes a picture of me. I have it in my house.

And he tells me, we can bring this here! To the camp. You know. OK, so what for, I say. And he laughs at me. Laughs! What for? Why would you live without it?

How long have we known each other, Constantine? How long, eh? A long time! I can tell you the pegs in this table. You remember? Steady as a rock I held it. You, hammering away while she was cooking? Out there. In the spring. That door! There isn't a thing in this house doesn't have my fingerprints on it.

Look at you now, yes. Look how you are living. (RESIGNED) I would ask you to come with us but… But the boy? Yes. Think about the boy? About Gethin. Without the Village? What have you got? The forests to hunt in. (GESTURING TO THE RABBITS) The odd set to still dig up? Without the camp, how long do you think you can survive up here, eh? With nothing. No money? Can't trap bottles!

CONSTANTINE (MENACINGLY) He stays. You go!

REMUS studies him, then shrugs.

REMUS   Your world. (HE THINKS ABOUT LEAVING) What do you want me to tell Timian?

CONSTANTINE Tell him what you like.

REMUS   He will want compensation. I promised I'd talk to you.

CONSTANTINE   What does he want?

REMUS   He's Timian. An apology from you would not go amiss but... Well, high horses will fly before that happens. (BEAT) I'll take one of the rabbits.

He rises, heading for the rabbits. CONSTANTINE grabs his arm. REMUS pauses.

CONSTANTINE   The bottle!

REMUS thinks about challenging him, then acquiesces and reaches into a pocket. He thumbs through a few coins and deposits the minor ones on the table. CONSTANTINE releases his arm.

REMUS goes to the rabbits and selects one, cutting the cord that binds it to the others.

REMUS   She would have hated to see you like this, Constantine. The man you've become? Independence... We understand independence but this... Think about it. He is barely more than an urchin now. Where would he be without the Village!

          Think about it, OK?

CONSTANTINE moves over to the door, ready to open it. REMUS wraps himself in preparation for the cold.

REMUS (cont.)   Think about it.

CONSTANTINE opens the door just enough for REMUS to squeeze through, which he does. CONSTANTINE struggles to close the door again.

GETHIN stays where he is.

The door closed, CONSTANTINE goes to the rabbits. He takes one over to the table and, grabbing the knife from where he'd left it on the table, he beheads it and begins to skin it.

Slowly, cautiously, GETHIN rises and goes over to the stove. He goes unwatched by CONSTANTINE as he picks up the snow that has seeped in and puts it into the fire.

He relaxes slightly and makes his way back across the room towards his bed.

As he passes CONSTANTINE lashes out, hitting the boy in the face and sending him to the ground. The sudden casualness of the action is shocking but the old man never looks at the fallen boy who has blood running from his nose.

The boy, inert on the floor, waits for further reprisals but the old man continues with the skinning.

Slowly, cautiously, the boy rises. From within his ragged clothes he pulls some bread he has stolen.

Gingerly, as if approaching a wild animal, he holds out the bread and puts it on the table, all the time expecting another hit.

A potato comes the same way, then a carrot. He waits for his father's approval.

With the rabbit skinned, CONSTANTINE looks at the money on the table, then at the produce. He upends the knife and drives it deep into the table.

FADE TO BLACK.

END OF ACT 1.

ACT 2

ACT 2

It is night time in the cabin.

Outside the snow storm has stopped, but the howl of the wind continues to shake the room.

A fresh full moon shines in through the window. A thick candle is the only other light. The room is filled with ominous shadows and dark corners.

On the stove is a pot containing rabbit stew.

CONSTANTINE, drunk, is sitting on his bed in a state of mild undress. A bottle is clutched carelessly in his hand.

At his feet GETHIN is trying to get his boots off.

The old man is singing, sadly, almost internally.

CONSTANTINE   Five hundred sons my hand ran through / Five hundred hands from
me to you / Five hundred widows at the grave / Five hundred times this soul I gave. / Five hundred sons my hand did end / Five hundred

times to make amends / Five hundred men that
I saw die / The last of the five hundred: I!

His father's feet free, GETHIN moves to take
the bottle. Again the old man swings out catching the boy violently, but this one is expected
and the boy barely pauses as he moves to aid
the old man back onto his bed.

Immediately the old man breaks into a rhyth-
mic snore.

GETHIN turns to the table and deposits the
candle, blowing it out.

The knife is still stuck in the table and, check-
ing that the old man cannot see him, he takes it
before he makes his way to his own bed in the
opposite corner.

The two men are drowned in shadows. Only
the wind and moonlight remain.

The old man chokes and wakes.

Pause.

GETHIN   Who was that brought me
to the house?

CONSTANTINE Sleep.

GETHIN   Who was that brought me

here.

CONSTANTINE   No one. No one. None of them!

GETHIN   He knew ma?

CONSTANTINE   None of them!

GETHIN   You knew him

CONSTANTINE   Yes

GETHIN   I knew him?

CONSTANTINE   Many times. He used to come here.

GETHIN   I don't know that.

CONSTANTINE   Always caught you.

GETHIN   I don't know that. (PAUSE) How old was I?

CONSTANTINE   Why?

GETHIN   I don't remember him.

Silence.

CONSTANTINE   Tell me. (SILENCE) Tell me!

Outside a wolf howls. Another answers.

GETHIN   Close.

CONSTANTINE   Tell me.

GETHIN   (RECITING) They came from the east.

CONSTANTINE   Yes.

GETHIN   Course of them.

CONSTANTINE   Yes.

A wolf howls.

GETHIN   She was the most beautiful creature he had seen, this land or another.

CONSTANTINE   Eyes like…

GETHIN   Eyes like sapphire. She wore a white dress and hair in red. Steepled like a beggars' hands.

A wolf howls. CONSTANTINE answers with one of his own.

GETHIN (cont.)   They were married under the tree – the fire tree – down at the end of the camp. Only it wasn't the fire tree then. It was just a tree. The fire tree would come later.

CONSTANTINE   She wore green!

GETHIN   Yes.

CONSTANTINE   And her hands were so cold!

GETHIN   You buried yourselves under the water, by the fire tree, in the river, the bear high above you. Great bear! Cupped in moonlight.

A wolf starts to howl. CONSTANTINE joins it in chorus. GETHIN waits for them to finish before going on.

GETHIN (cont.)   You buried yourselves for the whole Village to watch, and when you rose, under the bear, the whole Village carried you back to the tavern.

CONSTANTINE   Green.

GETHIN   And then they came.

CONSTANTINE   Yes.

GETHIN   Not that night. Not the night after. The great bear moved on. Orion's belt measured the pair of you. (PAUSE) And you (BEAT) gloried in each other. Gorged each other. Like wild animals mount, you mounted. (BEAT) And everyone cheered.

CONSTANTINE   Yes.

GETHIN   And then they came. Kind like. Inside the camp. Right under your very own doorstep.

CONSTANTINE   Right there.

GETHIN   And they devoured the Village. Monsters of men! Blood handed from the bottomless slain. They tore at the very shred of us. Of all of us! Of children!

Another howl from outside. This time there is no response.

GETHIN (cont.)   Cousin against cousin. End against end. They came over the ridge and saw the camp and the lake beyond it, and waded into us.

Pause.

GETHIN (cont.)   No man could stand against them. Some… fled. Others fell. They cut and they chewed and they gave no edge for hope.

And so they called him. They called you. And you were deep in love. Buried. Warm. And they dug you up with their calling. Sought you out. The Village, red with blood, light with fire. They called to you and you stretched and you answered, as you always answered, as you had always answered.

And so you bathed. And you spent hammer on metal. And you clothed yourself for war. (BEAT) And you left her.

CONSTANTINE   Yes.

GETHIN   With new life inside her, you left her. (PAUSE) And the plain was burning. High as a horse it was burning but you cut through it. Cut through it to crash into the camp.

What you saw there! The whispers of men! Old enemies licking like dogs the feet that had down trod them. Friends turned black with blood, shading themselves with the clothes of their conquerors.

And so you cut them! You! Under Orion's belt you cut them! Best and the worst. Hundreds deep!

And you laid them at your feet, gripping their flesh with your toes until the ground they fought on was no more than entrails!

Fled or fallen. Fled or fallen they leave. The men of the east exorcised from the Village.

How long have you gloried in the blood of your enemies? How long have you carried the weight of the camp? Long enough for life to come beyond the ridge. Long enough for baby's cries to rattle these walls. (SOTTO, HIS OWN ADDITION) Long enough for these lungs.

A long wolf howl, far away. CONSTANTINE is silent. Asleep once more.

Pause.

Almost unseen in the dark, moving slowly to avoid any noise, GETHIN has moved himself into a seated position on the edge of the bed.

In his hand he holds the knife.

GETHIN (cont.)   She was gone. When you returned. Like the air gone. The baby lying on the bed where he had her. Warm in her blood.

The old man is asleep. The boy listening for his breathing hears a snore just before a wolf howls.

GETHIN rises, tucking the knife out of sight of the moonlight.

The wind, rising, rattles the door and the boy uses it to mask his movements as he tiptoes across to the sleeping old man, knife in hand, purpose clear.

He is almost on him when the wind blows the door open, flooding the room with moonlight.

The boy falls on the old man, trying to force the knife to his throat, but the old man has woken and is rising.

He clenches the boy's arm as it pushes for his throat.

The boy puts his weight behind it but it's not enough. The old man twists the arm down and head-butts the boy.

The knife spins away onto the floor and the boy flails backwards, skidding behind the lost knife.

GETHIN (cont.)   No!

But the old man is on him, his hands at his throat.

A wolf howls, close now. Wind whips the stage.

The old man looks at the open, flapping door. He hits the boy brutally and drags him, half unconscious, to the threshold.

The boy starts to stir just in time to find himself thrown out into the snow.

He lets out a cry and rising struggles for the closing door, leaning his weight against it.

GETHIN (cont.)   No! Papa, no!

But the old man's anger is enough to conquer his son and the wind.

As it closes, a wolf howls.

Silence.

The old man leans against the door.

Then starts the banging. Loud crashes rock the door and the old man, who starts to fear the entire wall might fall.

GETHIN (cont.)   (LOUDLY OFF) Papa! Papa! Please! Papa!

Amidst the calls and bangs, the wolves start again, numerous voices loud, near and far. A cacophony drowning out even the pounding on the door.

GETHIN (cont.)   (LOUDLY OFF) Papa, papa! Open the door! Papa! Please! (ETC.)

CONSTANTINE   (SCREAMING) Tell it!

GETHIN   (LOUDLY   OFF)   Papa! (ETC.)

CONSTANTINE covers his ears against the noise

CONSTANTINE   Tell it!

GETHIN   (LOUDLY   OFF)   Papa!
Please! Please!

The howls of the wolves, the banging on the
door, the screams of his son, all reach a cre-
scendo, the old man nearly doubled over at the
noise.

CONSTANTINE   (SCREAMING)   Teeeeeel-
llllllll iiiiiiiittttt!

Silence.

No wolves. No banging. No cries.

Even the wind has dissipated.

The old man unfurls. He rises slowly, his back
to the door, listening for the sound of anything.

Suddenly, scared, he turns and opens the door.

GETHIN is lying in the snow behind the door.
Further out we see the green eyes of a pack of
wolves, mere feet away.

CONSTANTINE (cont.) Away   with   you!
Away!

He grabs the prone boy and drags him back
into the cabin, throwing him onto the floor before returning to the doorway.

Stretching out against the door lintels, he rages into the night.

CONSTANTINE (cont.) Away with you! You hear me! All of you!

The wind and wolves, as if answering, let out a cry. The old man is buffeted as he stands in the doorway, the first flakes of a new snow storm drifting in through the opening, catching in his hair and beard.

CONSTANTINE (cont.) I don't need you! You hear me! You hear me! Go! You want to go, go! I don't need you! You think I need you! I don't need any of you! Any of you! He's mine! Do you hear me? Mine! My blood! You want him? You want him? He's mine and I will do whatever with him! Whatever I want!

The wolves withdraw.

CONSTANTINE (cont.)   Come at me! Come at me, if you dare! I will end you! All of you! Come at me!

Only the wind buffets him now. Only the snow.

CONSTANTINE (cont.) He's mine, do you hear me? Mine! My blood! You want to go, go! All of you! But he! Is! Mine!

GETHIN is rising.

GETHIN   Papa!

CONSTANTINE   (OBLIVIOUS) Come at me if you're coming! I dare you! Come on! Come at me! What are you waiting for?

GETHIN goes to him and tries to pull him back into the house.

GETHIN   Papa! Please! Papa.

CONSTANTINE   Where are you, eh? Where are you?

GETHIN   Papa! Stop it! Please!

CONSTANTINE   Mine! You hear me!

GETHIN   Papa!

CONSTANTINE   Get off me!

GETHIN   Come back in!

CONSTANTINE   Get off me!

But the old man is acquiescing, allowing the boy to drag him back inside and together they start to close the door.

GETHIN   Papa…

CONSTANTINE   Push! God damn you!

They push the door shut, the snow picking up.

They stand there, wheezing. The old man looks at his son, both of them shivering in the cold.

He calmly, almost affectionately, delivers a backhand blow that sends the boy to the floor once more before proceeding to the table and the bottle.

CONSTANTINE   Tell it!

GETHIN remains silent. The old man drinks.

CONSTANTINE (cont.) (SOFTLY)   Tell   it, damn you.

GETHIN   (WEARY) They came from the east.

This time the old man's responses are in contrast. Strong. Full of pride.

CONSTANTINE   Yes.

GETHIN   Courses of them.

CONSTANTINE   Yes! (HE DRINKS, THEN FONDLY) Tell it!

GETHIN   She was the most beautiful creature he had seen, this land or another. Eyes like sapphire. She wore a white dress and hair in red. Steepled like a beggar's hands. They were married under the tree – the fire tree – down at the end of the camp. Only it wasn't the fire tree then. It was just a tree. The fire tree would come later. You buried yourselves under the water, by the fire tree, in the river, the bear high above you. Cupped in moonlight. You buried yourselves, for the whole camp to watch, and when you rose, the whole camp carried you back to the tavern.

As the story unfolds the boy curls himself into a ball from the cold and the old man drinks.

Clouds scour the moon casting the room into fits of blackness, increasing in darkness with every pass until finally the story is being told in complete obscurity.

GETHIN   And then they came.

END OF ACT 2.

ACT 3

ACT 3

Daytime.

Inside the house GETHIN is alone.

Outside the storm has abated.

He is struggling with the pot from the stove. Carrying it over to the table he removes the lid and, rolling up a sleeve, slides his hand into the broth, searching along the bottom.

He finds what he's looking for and pulls out a piece of bone. He picks the meat off, dropping it back into the stew, and then carefully sucks the bone dry before placing it on the table.

He does this several more times, fishing and finding as many bones as he can, never interested in the meat.

Through it all he keeps watch on the door.

Satisfied that there are no more bones to be found he pulls down his sleeve without wiping his arm, replaces the lid, and returns the pan to its place on the stove.

He scampers across to his bed and pulls out a box from a hidden position behind his mattress.

Returning to the table he opens the box and pulls out a knotted handkerchief. He opens it to reveal more bones of all sizes and a collection of odd string. Comparing the new bones to them he adds them to the collection before reaching into the box once more and returning with three or four sculptures.

He is making bone monsters. Delicate, incredibly crafted statues made out of bone and string, they stand on the table a mixture of craftsmanship, ingenuity and horror. They are beautiful and twisted: a cat's jaw on a mouse's spine, frog's legs with a human finger.

Creatively speaking, they are works of genius.

Before we do, he hears footsteps approaching and moves to put away the statues.

In his eagerness he knocks one off the table and, squealing in horror, is in the process of picking up the pieces when REMUS enters.

REMUS   Constantine!

He sees the boy and pauses.

REMUS   Constantine?

GETHIN   Out!

REMUS sees the sculptures and heads for them. GETHIN moves to block him, pawing at the man as he tries to approach.

REMUS   What've you got here?

GETHIN   No!

REMUS shrugs him off, his hand on the arm GETHIN had in the soup.

REMUS   Get off! (LOOKING AT HIS HAND) God, you're... filthy animal!

GETHIN backs off as if stung.

REMUS picks up one of the statues

REMUS (cont.)   What have we here?

GETHIN   Mine!

REMUS   (ANGERED) I'm not taking them. I'm just having a... You made these, did you? On your own? There's... Who taught you to do this, boy?

GETHIN   They're mine!

REMUS   There's... There's crafts-men...

REMUS spies something in the box and retrieves it. GETHIN tries to snatch it before he does but REMUS is too quick.

It is a photo. Old. Faded.

REMUS   Well, well! God, she was something! Look at her! A man could stand exile with something like that… Does he tell you about her, boy? Does he tell you what she was like?

GETHIN   Green.

REMUS   He was something to be feared in those days!

GETHIN   Mine!

REMUS   Nothing is ours boy. Best learn that.

The door opens revealing CONSTANTINE who enters carrying his bride.

Though not noticeably younger, he is clearly more vital, brimming with power despite his age.

AMERICA is young, far too young and beautiful for a man like him.

She is laughing.

CONSTANTINE   Woopsie! Here we go…

One, two…

She giggles.

On three the old man crosses the threshold. The hovel is suddenly bathed in warm sunlight. Cobwebs magically disappearing. Though still a hovel it is a warm, magical one.

The bride looks around and likes what she sees.

At the front of the stage GETHIN and REMUS disappear into the shadow of the table.

AMERICA   Oh, it's…

He drops her down, still full of vigour.

CONSTANTINE   Yes, not much, but home. Home! Let me look at you.

AMERICA   (PULLING AWAY PLAY-FULLY) No, I want to see it! (BEAT) Home!

CONSTANTINE   If you'll have me.

AMERICA starts to tour the room.

AMERICA   This… This is our bed? Our bed.

CONSTANTINE   Home.

AMERICA   Our stove?

CONSTANTINE   Something else to heat us!

AMERICA   (BEAT) Our table.

CONSTANTINE   Where I'll have you as well!

AMERICA   (TEASING) Aren't you too old for that?

CONSTANTINE   Meat on my bones.

AMERICA   You'll need a nap soon.

CONSTANTINE   I'll be running you through before that!

AMERICA   Have to catch me first!

They start to chase, AMERICA putting objects between them.

AMERICA (cont.) Catch me!

She puts a chair in front of him and he flicks it away with a roar, catching her arm and pulling her into him.

They kiss.

AMERICA (cont.) You won't miss it?

CONSTANTINE   What's mine to miss?

AMERICA   Castles, lands…

CONSTANTINE   Exploring to be done right here!

She squirms away in delight.

AMERICA   And if they come?

CONSTANTINE   I'll kill them!

AMERICA   And if they fight?

CONSTANTINE Cut   their   throats!   (HE GRABS HER) Take more than the lands to keep me from you.

Belieing his age he lifts her onto the table and the two fall about each other.

The old man is annoyed. No matter the passion, something is wrong. He fumbles at her, getting increasingly frustrated.

CONSTANTINE (cont.)   Damn it!

Beneath the table GETHIN covers his ears but REMUS stands and moves around the room watching them. When he gets near the door, he coughs and the couple turn around.

AMERICA   Remus!

CONSTANTINE (ANGERED) Bald   faced bastard!

AMERICA   No!

AMERICA stills him, breaks free.

AMERICA (cont.) None of that! You hear me? Remus is a friend. Your friend!

She hugs REMUS.

The two men eye each other.

AMERICA (cont.) Remus! It's good to see you again!

REMUS   (TO CONSTANTINE) So, you've returned?

CONSTANTINE   I have!

REMUS   No more lands for you?

AMERICA   Stop it! You are brothers! Once upon a time. And now!

CONSTANTINE   I'm hungry.

AMERICA   How are you Remus? Bronzed, it would seem.

REMUS   The Village is eager for you to join them, Constantine. We could use your arm, and your... wisdom.

CONSTANTINE   Fuck the Village! And fuck you, brother. Everything I need is here!

REMUS   No one is alone.

CONSTANTINE   Alone? Is that right? Do I

look alone? (To AMERICA) Get us bread!

The bride does as she is told.

REMUS   I'm sorry you feel like that, Constantine.

CONSTANTINE   What is it about men, hmm? Fuck us once and you think you can fuck us again. Is that it? I don't need the Village and it doesn't need me. Understand that? Can you get that into your thick skull? Hmm? Far as I'm concerned, you can all burn!

REMUS   Is that what it taught you?

CONSTANTINE   Hmm? What was that?

REMUS   Is that what it taught you? Over the lake?

CONSTANTINE   Take care with your tone!

REMUS   No, I don't think I will!

AMERICA   Stop it! Both of you! Husband... Remus, you are... always welcome here. Always! This was your home!

CONSTANTINE   Like fuck it was!

AMERICA   Husband! (TO REMUS) You are always welcome here. (TO HER HUSBAND) There's no water. (HE DOESN'T

HEAR) Husband? Water!

CONSTANTINE   What's that?

AMERICA   There's no water. Not here.

CONSTANTINE   So?

AMERICA   You might get some… for our guest. Unless you want him to drink all the wine?

CONSTANTINE   Fucker's staying that long?

AMERICA   Enough! Water! Please.

CONSTANTINE   (GLARING AT REMUS) Fine!

They watch him exit. Silence as REMUS looks around the cabin, AMERICA stands with her back against the table watching her husband depart down the hill for the water.

REMUS picks up a metal poker.

AMERICA   Do you miss it?

REMUS   Hmm?

AMERICA   I would, I think. Had I grown up here.

REMUS   As many bad memories as good.

AMERICA   Was he rough with you? At the end.

REMUS   All men are rough. It's in our nature.

AMERICA   (FLIRTING) He is with me.

REMUS stops, looks at her.

AMERICA   (cont.) You are right about him.

REMUS   What am I right about him?

AMERICA   What you're thinking.

REMUS   What am I thinking?

AMERICA   How long over the lake was he. How many children.

REMUS   I wouldn't know.

AMERICA   But you're thinking it.

REMUS   I think many things.

AMERICA   I'm glad to hear it!

Silence

AMERICA (cont.) The well pum…

REMUS   When I lived here… When I was young with him… I picked up this before.

It's not this one, but he taught me how to make it. Taught me how to make it, bending metal over and over in a furnace. Over and over, and then he'd hit me with it. Not a man to cross.

He is nearer her now.

AMERICA   The well pump is broken.

They stare at each other.

REMUS   America…

AMERICA   Hush!

Swiftly REMUS reaches out and pulls back her hair, his mouth inches from hers. She doesn't resist.

AMERICA (cont.) It's alright.

He mounts her quickly, as much in anger as passion. She pulls him into her.

REMUS   Tell me you love me!

Silence.

REMUS (cont.)   Tell me!

But there is no response. And she buries his mouth in hers to silence him.

Their coupling is quick and powerful. As he finishes she pulls him in deeply.

Sated he leans into her and she strokes his hair.

AMERICA   (AS IF TO A CHILD) There. Hush… It's over now… Hush. Hush.

Hearing this he pulls away, covering himself as he does.

AMERICA (cont.) You have names for me?

REMUS   Come with me!

AMERICA   (LAUGHING) Do you imagine? No. You are beautiful Remus. He will be a fantastic boy!

REMUS   I don't understand you.

AMERICA   Go out the back way now. Pumps don't stay broken.

REMUS   Come with me.

AMERICA   They have bluebird where I come from. Not like here. Blue. Birds. With actual blue feathers and… They look so pretty, in the sky, flying above you. Out of reach. But these birds. You know, you can take the feathers of a bird, any bird, and make the best poisons in the world. All of them. Grind down the feathers, dry the powder. Why is that, you think? That they are so poisonous to men? But these blue birds. Delicious! You bake them, roast some chestnuts in their stomachs. Some rosemary…. You have to pluck them carefully of course. Nothing is more poisonous than their feathers, but delicious.

Look after yourself, Remus. Look after him if you live.

He looks at her.

AMERICA (cont.) Now. Go!

REMUS crosses past her to an unseen exit downstage.

As he passes she reaches out and digs her nails into his arm, marking him.

AMERICA (cont.) That is to remember me by!

She scratches deep into his arm. He twists away in pain and stares at her in bewilderment.

AMERICA (cont.) Now go!

REMUS returns to his position next to GETH-IN.

AMERICA sits, quietly. Sad but with a sense of accomplishment.

Outside her husband calls.

CONSTANTINE   (OFF) Wife!

She looks up. Goes to the door.

CONSTANTINE (cont.) (OFF) Wife.

She pauses, then moves out after him.

AMERICA   What are we mewling now, husband?

Exit AMERICA.

Lights up on REMUS and GETHIN.

The cabin has returned to its state of disrepair, the memories of the past extinguished.

REMUS is holding one of the bone monsters up to the light. GETHIN looks at him as if he was holding his soul.

REMUS   Read, can you?

The boy shakes his head.

REMUS (cont.)   Numbers?

Another shake.

REMUS (cont.)   Rag of a boy, aren't you? What are these things?

GETHIN gently takes the sculpture back.

GETHIN   They live beyond the lake.

REMUS   That right?

The boy starts taking the animals one by one from the box and shows them to the fascinated and repulsed REMUS.

GETHIN   Over the lake they taxes them. Words. You speak and you get taxed.

They got... This one... He is the great speaker, right. An'... And he uses lots of words and so they taxes him. They taxes him so he can't use the word no more. An' the words... The words, they get angry at this cos taxes are bad, aren't they. So they get angry at this and they don't come no more, the words, and this one... This one... He's got to speak, right. For the Village... He's got to speak but the words don't come no more because they be taxed and don't like it. (PAUSE) That's why they don't come no more. Across the lake. Words.

Pause.

REMUS   Had a horse like you. Once. Good legs. Strong. Mind like a fig. Stood hands above the rest of them! Every bone in his body muscled perfectly. Could I train it? I could not! Thousand times round the harness and every time like the first. (PAUSE) Still wouldn't be the first time.

Enter CONSTANTINE.

This time when CONSTANTINE enters the snow whips the room. There is no sunlight to greet him.

All three cower from the wind and drive, GETHIN hunching quickly over his statues, focused on getting them back into the box before CONSTANTINE notices.

CONSTANTINE struggles with the door, using all his efforts to close it once more behind the sudden snow storm.

The storm is getting worse.

The door secured, he shakes snow from his mane and sees REMUS at the table.

He pauses. In his hand a pail of iced water is set down, and he adjusts his knife as he speaks.

CONSTANTINE   Again?

REMUS   I thought to give you one last chance. (HE BRUSHES SNOW FROM HIS HAIR) You'll be buried soon.

CONSTANTINE takes the pail to the stove and then moves across to the table.

He pulls a root vegetable from his cloak. It is frozen but he begins hacking at it with his knife as he watches his old adversary in love.

Carefully REMUS sits down near him. GETH-IN scuttles to hide his box. The two glance at him.

CONSTANTINE   Find what you want?

REMUS   Timian wants him. For the shop. In fact he… What he says… He owns him, for the stealing.

CONSTANTINE begins to gnaw on the strips of vegetable.

CONSTANTINE   Been paid.

REMUS   One rabbit is not… It appears to be more than that, the theft. Timian… He does not want people involved. Your good name…. He says he wants to take the boy. With him. Across the lake. He will train him, give him purpose. This he promises. Fit punishment, I think. You can come too.

CONSTANTINE   Boy stays.

Silence.

REMUS   I ever tell you about the

boat, Constantine?

CONSTANTINE   More stories, Remus?

Suddenly alive, REMUS produces a flask from inside his coat.

REMUS   Meh, the snow is too strong to go out. Look, for us! One last drink between friends? Old friends, OK? One last story.

The old man watches him as he looks for cups.

REMUS   The Village is nearly packed, Constantine. Mid-morning, tomorrow. Day after, depending on the storms. Soon we will be gone, eh? Out of your hair? Unless you change your mind..? No, I can see not. Still one last drink. One last story for old friends.

He puts three cups on the table. Instantly CONSTANTINE picks one up and throws it across the room at GETHIN who ducks out of its way.

REMUS is incensed and reaches inside his clothes, presumably for a weapon. CONSTANTINE glares at him.

CONSTANTINE   Not for him!

REMUS thinks, then shrugs. His earlier mask of effusion returning. He pours.

REMUS   Fine, fine. You treat him too hard, Constantine. Always have. Boy is wild in all but name. But, your son. Your son. I told Timian as much. You cannot make him give up his son, I told him. Yes, he steals. Yes, he owes you, but the other side of the lake…? This is too much. I told him this!

CONSTANTINE   The boat?

REMUS   (CONFUSED) Sorry?

CONSTANTINE   You were telling me about the boat?

REMUS   Oh. Yes. Well… I cannot tell you about the boat! You know all about the boat! Who but you, eh? No. Still. This time… I have not taken the boat like you have, Constantine. All that back and fore, back and fore! Days were you lived on the boat, did you not? No, I have… Once or twice, no more. So, for me, it is still a big adventure, yes? When we sail, when the Village crosses, big adventure! But, that is now. This is then. Much then. I… You had just returned. A year, tops, and I thought of you. I did! I thought, Constantine crossed the lake. Why not I? Yes! So I crossed. You know what this is like.

He pauses. Drinks.

REMUS (cont.)   You remember before the lightning? You remember that? How the world changes, eh. How were we so wrong? I ask you that. Seriously. For so long, so wrong. How can that be? Expansion, yes? This is all we talked about. Those nights by the fire, when we built this place. This table, eh? Expansion! The Village!

          Where to next, that's what we used to ask ourselves. So simple. So simple! Where to next. We were… whirlwinds! Whirlwinds! Now here, now here!

He tops the old man's drink.

REMUS (cont.)   Now where are we? Hmm? We reached everything. Everything! And… Yes, when we got there, but… Expansion. That was what we talked about. Expansion. Now? Who wants expansion anymore? Who wants all the bother? Give us lightning! This is what we ask. Give us lightning!

          Small worlds full of lightning.

          When you came back…

When you brought her here… You were my idol! You know that? Expansion! Then you came back.

He drinks.

CONSTANTINE   The boat.

REMUS   Right. Yes. So, well, you came back and I thought, why not! So I took the boat. And then, right there… I saw it, Constantine. I saw it! Lights in the darkness, that's all we are! Pinpricks of lights! I stood there, on the deck, and I'm looking out at… nothing. Nothing! No stars, no sea, nothing! Blackness and then I see it. This light. Tiny, ahead of me. And I hold up my thumb, just so, and I hold it, and the light goes. (HE MOVES HIS THUMB) Light, no light. Light, no light.

Hours I do this. Hours. Light, no light. And at times, I think the light is bigger. Sometimes it fits around my thumb and then it's nothing again, banished by a digit. Banished.

But, little by little, it grows. A ship. Naturally. Moving towards and away at the same time. Towards and away.

Saddest thing I've ever seen.

CONSTANTINE takes the flask and empties the contents into his cup.

REMUS   We were... It was the only way we could be proud. The only way... We used to be about the expansion of the Village. Now we are only about the expansion of ourselves.

CONSTANTINE downs the rest of his drink and rises, done.

REMUS (cont.).   You have to let him go, Constantine.

CONSTANTINE swings out an arm and catches REMUS, sending him back off his chair.

REMUS is unprepared for the attack and spins ungainly onto the floor, scampering for a grip.

CONSTANTINE roars and tosses away the table with surprising power.

In the corner GETHIN screams and covers his face.

CONSTANTINE (ROARING) He is mine! Mine! Never, never will he be yours, do you hear me? Never!

REMUS   I'm ... Have no...

CONSTANTINE Take your hordes! Take them. You see me stopping you? But he is mine, do you hear me. To do as I will!

REMUS is on all fours, a knife drawn ahead of him.

REMUS   Cut you!

CONSTANTINE   Do it then. Do it!

He bears his chest, egging the man on. In the corner GETHIN giggles.

The wind howls. A window breaks. The storm rages outside. Snow pours in through the hole. Both men turn to protect themselves from the driving snow and wind.

In the corner GETHIN screams.

The old man pulls his shirt around him again to protect from the cold.

REMUS rises, the knife still in front of him. He has to scream through the wind to make himself heard.

REMUS   She would not have liked this! She would not have you! He is hers! Do you hear me? Not mine! Not yours! Hers.

The knife in front of him still, he exits.

The door stays open. Snow is drifting in now, pouring into the room like water as we fade to black.

END OF ACT 3.

ACT 4

ACT 4

SCENE 1

The past. The room as it was. Snow pulled through the broken window is piled over everything, but the storm is gone and the room is bathed in the summer tones of the past.

AMERICA, heavily pregnant. She stands at the table, feeling the baby inside her kick. She is singing a lullaby.

AMERICA   Song birds, to parchment / sorrow songs to pillow-cases / Someone's departed, you become the broken hearted / Faces crack, summers lack, songs turn to chore / This is what we're looking after…

          Kindness, to closed hands / Oaks turn to fire starters / King's crowns all fall down / You become another martyr /Hunger comes, rabbits run, water turns to hue / This is what we're looking after, this is what is coming after…

Song birds, to parchment...

The old man enters, girding himself for war. The armour is old and worn, almost ridiculous.

AMERICA stops singing and watches him as he bends and retrieves a sword wrapped in oil cloth from underneath the bed.

Ignoring her he takes it to the table and begins carefully to unwrap it.

AMERICA (cont.) I don't like this.

CONSTANTINE Nor I.

AMERICA The baby is close. I feel him.

Silence.

AMERICA (cont.) It's not your fight.

CONSTANTINE No.

AMERICA Then stay.

CONSTANTINE Don't bite me woman! If the Village falls...

AMERICA We are not the Village.

CONSTANTINE Married there.

AMERICA How many times...

CONSTANTINE Stop biting at me. (Pause)

It's decided.

AMERICA   And the baby?

CONSTANTINE   You are more than capable.

Silence.

AMERICA.   (FINALLY   EXPLODING)
You... You... Old man! You would rather war
than arms around me? Hold your son?

CONSTANTINE   He is mine. He will understand.

AMERICA   With winter... With winter
closing every day, this is what you would rather do? This is where you would rather be? You...
Old man! Do you think it will make you young
again? Is that it, old man? Blood on your hands
will make you young again? And how will you
scare them? With your beard? Your pot belly?
Are these the tools of war now? Is this what it's
come to? Do young men look down from their
horses, see a shuffling old goat and piss themselves? Coming towards them with a pig stick-
er and think the end is near? Is that it?

          Do they shudder at the sight
of decrepitude and dream of surrender?

CONSTANTINE   I'll be back before winter.

AMERICA   You'll be back on your bed. Laid out bloody before me while your enemies sate themselves on me. On our child! (HE IS READY TO GO) Others would not leave me. You think the men of the Village would leave such a prize?

CONSTANTINE   Good, then. If I'm gone.

AMERICA   There are those that would have me.

CONSTANTINE   There are those who'd have peace if it were offered them.

AMERICA   Leave now and he is not yours.

CONSTANTINE (ROUNDING ON HER) Where would you have me stand, woman! With my tail between my legs? In irons at your feet? Son or no, that is my blood and he will understand if I come back on a bed or no.

AMERICA   Perhaps.

Silence.

CONSTANTINE. Perhaps?

AMERICA   Fight your war then.

CONSTANTINE   Say it again.

AMERICA   It was nothing.

CONSTANTINE   What was nothing.

AMERICA   Go then. See if…

CONSTANTINE   Perhaps?

AMERICA   You've made your decision.

Silence.

CONSTANTINE   That bald faced bastard!

AMERICA   No!

CONSTANTINE   Him, or another?

AMERICA   Husband…

CONSTANTINE   I should gut you!

AMERICA   The child is yours! I feel it!

CONSTANTINE   Aye, but you thought you'd make sure! Is that it?

AMERICA   I was scared.

CONSTANTINE   Ten thousand men may fall at my feet but I'll count them none until his blood is on me!

AMERICA   Husband…

He flings his arm, hitting her around the face carelessly. She falls in a heap, silent, and looks at him. He turns and marches out the door.

AMERICA (cont.) Husband!

She starts to stand, and then staggers back clutching her stomach in pain.

AMERICA (cont.) Husband!

She puts her hand down between her legs and it comes up bloody. She goes to move to the doorway and a sharp pain sends her clutching to the floor. She screams.

AMERICA (cont.) No, no, no, no, no! Not now!

She starts to shift position and another shard of pain drives her to the floor.

She is going into labour. The blood is clear and visible on her dress and the floor. She is breathing fast. Her face and arms covered in sweat and blood. In between contractions she turns herself to a sitting position on the floor and spreads her legs.

Each new contraction is stronger than the last, the blood now pooling from between her legs.

AMERICA (cont.)   Come... Come on, then... Come on! You little bastard. You little shit. Come on, then. Come...

A contraction drives her back and she screams out again. Her hand reaching between her legs as she feels the baby crowning.

AMERICA (cont.) (IN TEARS) Fuck you, then. Fuck... You little shit. You little shit! I'm gonna...

She pushes hard driving the baby out of her. She screams. It falls with a thud between her legs and lies there. She falls back. The blood begins to pool once more.

All is still.

Then the baby cries.

AMERICA is raised by it.

She pulls herself to the table, the baby dragged along by the cord. She reaches up, takes the knife and cuts the cord. She never once touches the child.

Struggling, she rises. The baby is screaming on the floor. Steadying herself and bleeding badly, she steps over her child to the doorway.

The wind is picking up and it gusts snow outside.

She pauses, steadying herself, then steps out.

AMERICA (cont.) CONSTANTINE!

Exit AMERICA.

The wind picks up to the tune of the baby's cries, and snow gusts in the door covering the bloody trail AMERICA left upon exiting. The only sight in the room now is the baby lying, crying in a pool of snow and its mother's blood.

Day turns to night.

CONSTANTINE returns.

The baby has quietened. The storm abated.

He stands at the door, bloody but triumphant from the battle and looks at his child lying in a pool of blood.

Taking the cloak from his back he moves to the child and collects him in its folds.

FADE OUT.

END OF SCENE 1.

SCENE 2

CONSTANTINE is sitting alone at the table.

The storm is at its zenith now. Snow piles in every corner. The door shakes and rattles. Flakes swirl throughout the stage.

REMUS enters. Squeezing in through the doorway he pins it shut with his body before turning his attention to the old man who has not moved.

From beneath his heavy coat, REMUS removes a box.

The box, no bigger than A4 in size, is an ordinary looking wooden box, but this is the lightning box, holder of all power, and it is treated as such by the men.

From the doorway REMUS, hesitant to enter, watches the old man.

REMUS   Constantine.

CONSTANTINE   You have it.

REMUS   I do. Though what...

CONSTANTINE   Drink?

REMUS   I think you'll stab me, no.

CONSTANTINE   Just drink.

Pause.

REMUS   Alright then.

He sits at the table and puts the box on the table. Both men look at it while CONSTANTINE pours a drink.

CONSTANTINE   That's it?

REMUS   It is.

They drink. They refill.

CONSTANTINE   I ... I don't remember being young. I was once but... Memory is the death of you. You know this? It eats and it eats. As a young man it is... It is a kernel... This tiny side of you. And then it grows. No stopping it. (Beat) You begin to think. When you get older, you begin to think... And all that's there is memory. Memory on memory. Crushing. (HE DRINKS AND REFILLS) This doesn't help. So... Fuck it. Memory wins! Give up on today. Give up on it. Let the here and now... Wallow. (Pause) It does what you say?

REMUS   It does.

CONSTANTINE   God, she loved me. If she'd have seen me, coming back like that.... Vigour.

REMUS   You were... Young again.

CONSTANTINE   Last gasps of an old man. (BEAT) But with this...

The door is blown open, forced virtually off its hinges by the blizzard, and snow swirls around the room. The men cover to protect themselves. CONSTANTINE rises to close the door but GETHIN enters, a dead and frozen bird in his hands and manages to close it as much as is humanly possible against the driving snow.

The snow settles before anyone speaks.

GETHIN   I thought he don't come here no more.

CONSTANTINE   Get your things.

GETHIN holds up the small bird as if it were a prize.

REMUS   The Village is leaving, boy. You're coming with us.

GETHIN looks at CONSTANTINE.

CONSTANTINE   Get your things.

GETHIN   No.

REMUS   Boy...

CONSTANTINE   It's done.

The storm increases. The walls rattle. The door hammers at its hinges. Snow pours in through the broken window.

GETHIN   No!

REMUS   Listen to me boy...

GETHIN is beside himself. He shakes and begins to make whining noises which increase in intensity.

CONSTANTINE   Boy...

REMUS   Your father and...

CONSTANTINE   Listen to me boy...

In a swift move GETHIN flings the frozen bird at REMUS. He is shaking wildly now, rocking from side to side, the noises increasing, doing battle with the storm.

REMUS ducks the bird, unsure what to be more frightened of, the boy or the storm that is threatening to break the house.

REMUS   God... Constantine....

With a roar GETHIN flings himself at the man. A small rotten blade flashes in his hand. REMUS catches the knife arm just before it skewers him, but can do nothing about the other flailing appendages that batter him as the boy screams over the wind.

The sound of the two men's momentary battle is almost drowned out by the storm.

CONSTANTINE brings the butt of his knife down on the back of the boy's head and he crumples to the floor, unmoving.

The storm abates slightly.

REMUS rises.

CONSTANTINE   Take him and go.

REMUS seems to have come to his senses. He looks around the cabin as if seeing it for the first time.

REMUS   Constantine...

But the old man turns away, his attention on the box on the table.

CONSTANTINE   Bind him if you value your eyes.

REMUS thinks about saying something but refrains. He pulls the dead weight of the boy up and hoists him on his shoulders.

The old man ignores him, his attention solidly on the box.

The room is shaking now, the storm threatening to tear it apart. At the door REMUS pauses and looks back at the old man alone at the table, the box in front of him.

He calls out.

REMUS   It's just memory. Come with us!

It's not clear if the old man has heard him or not and he calls again.

REMUS (cont.)   CONSTANTINE!   Come with us!

But there is no reply. Bracing himself, REMUS opens the door and struggles through into the storm, the unconscious boy slung over his shoulder.

The storm picks up. The door blows in.

The other window breaks and snow swirls over the stage, pushing in through every crevice.

The old man never moves.

Caught in a snowstorm, drifts piling up around his ankles, the old man opens the lightning box. An electronic warm glow radiates from within, lighting the old man's face as he is forever lost in an eternal white-out.

He watches the light as we lose him in the snow storm. An old man, alone with his memories, dying from the cold.

CURTAIN

THE END

THOMAS ALEXANDER

Also by

THOMAS ALEXANDER

THOMAS ALEXANDER

THE VISITOR

THE VISITOR

BY

THOMAS ALEXANDER

WHEN THE LOVER OF A FAMOUS WRITER GOES MISSING IN A WAR RAVAGED COUNTRY, HE BRIBES HIS WAY INTO A JAIL TO QUESTION HER HUSBAND, A MISSIONARY, WHO IS BEING TORTURED AS A TRAINING EXERCISE BY HIS CAPTORS.

ALONE IN THE CELL, THE TWO START A DIALOGUE ABOUT THE NATURE OF BELIEF.

BELIEF IN GOD, LOVE AND POLITICS.

MURDER ME GENTLY

By

THOMAS ALEXANDER

"ONE MAN... ONE WOMAN... AND THE QUEST FOR JUSTICE IN AN UNJUST WORLD"

MODERN DAY RUSSIA THROUGH THE MEDIUM OF FILM NOIR

BLENDING REAL LIFE EVENTS WITH COMEDY AND INTRIGUE, **MURDER ME GENTLY**'S UNIQUE PERSPECTIVE ON THE WORLD OF RUSSIAN POLITICS AS SEEN THROUGH THE LENS OF FILM NOIR, SPANS THE ASSASSINATION OF INTERNATIONALLY RENOWNED JOURNALISTS, PUTIN'S REACH FOR THE RETURN OF SOVIET SATELLITE STATES, AND THE INFILTRATION OF GOVERNMENT BY OLIGARCHS AND CRIMINALS.

PROVIDING A DAMMING INDICTMENT OF THE WEST'S INABILITY TO HALT MOSCOW'S POLICY OF EXPANSIONISM **MURDER ME GENTLY** LENDS A THEATRICAL EXPOSE TO THE VERY REAL WORLD OF CORRUPTION AND GREED IN INTERNATIONAL POLITICS TODAY.

A CONMAN, A DISGRACED INTERPOL AGENT, A MAFIA BOSS, A CIA SPOOK, AND THE SECRET TO THE FUTURE ALL UNITE IN AN UNLIKELY ALLIANCE IN A LOVE AFFAIR THAT WILL DEFINE THE FATE OF THE WORLD IN THOMAS ALEXANDER'S

... MURDER ME ... GENTLY!

GRE⩓T

GREAT

BY

THOMAS ALEXANDER

A REMOTE ROOM IN THE THROWS OF WINTER.

THE ONCE GREAT MAN LIVES ALONE NOW WITH HIS SON,

AN OLD FRIEND HAS COME TO VISIT. HE HAS CLIMBED UP FROM THE VILLAGE IN ORDER TO OFFER THE OLD MAN ONE LAST CHANCE TO ESCAPE THE ENCROACHING WINTER THAT IS ABOUT TO TAKE HIM, STIRRING UP MEMORIES OF BETTER TIMES AND THE WARMTH OF SUMMER.

BEGAT

BY

THOMAS ALEXANDER

In a country, after the war, a Judge throws a dinner party, seeking support against a powerful minister who has raped and killed a servant girl.

But the Judge himself is the target tonight, and the shadow of the war he so desperately wants to leave behind threatens to engulf his family as a young woman seeks revenge for the sins of his past.

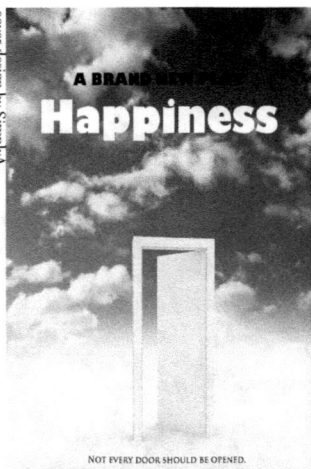

A BRAND NEW

Happiness

NOT EVERY DOOR SHOULD BE OPENED.

HAPPINESS

BY

THOMAS ALEXANDER

ON A REMOTE HEADLAND IN NORTH WALES A MAN AND HIS PARAPLEGIC SON DREAM OF LIFE BEYOND THE CONFINES OF THEIR FOUR WALLS.

BUT WHEN A WOMAN OFFERS THEM THE ESCAPE THEY SO CRAVE THEY FIND THEY ARE BOUND BY MORE THEN THEIR DREAMS.

THE JEALOUSY OF A BORED POLICE-MAN AND THE KINDNESS OF A MAIL ORDER BRIDE SET THEM ON A PATH OF HOPE AND DESTRUCTION.

THE LAST CHRISTMAS

BY

THOMAS ALEXANDER

THE LAST CHRISTMAS

IT'S NEWS!

WHEN AN EMBATTLED NEWSROOM RECEIVES A POTENTIALLY EARTH SHATTERING STORY MINUTES BEFORE AIR ON CHRISTMAS DAY THE CAREFUL EQUILIBRIUM OF THE TEAM IS SHATTERED AND OLD DIVIDING LINES COME TO THE FORE, TURNING CO-WORKER AGAINST CO-WORKER.

SET IN REAL TIME AND INCORPORATING ACTUAL AND INTERCHANGEABLE NEWS EVENTS THE LAST CHRISTMAS PITS SOCIAL POLITICS AGAINST JOURNALISTIC INTEGRITY IN A BATTLE OF THE ETHICS.

GOD

By

Thomas Alexander

When the named partner of a small law firm dies, leaving large debt, the remaining misfits of the firm are forced to take on just about any client available, including a litigious soccer-mum who would like to sue God for the death of her husband – hit by a lightning bolt on the 15th hole of a municipal golf course.

The Trial becomes complicated however, when an indigent with no background and a canny knack of knowing everyone's background enters the courtroom claiming to be 'God'.

Batting back and fore between the courtroom and the personal lives of the lawyers, 'God' is a fast paced courtroom drama/comedy that uses original staging and non-linear storytelling to provide a light-hearted, but complex social drama.

THE FAMILY

BY

THOMAS ALEXANDER

TODAY, FOR THE FIRST TIME IN LONGER THAN ANYONE CAN REMEMBER, THE FAMILY ARE GATHERING. THEY ARE GATHERING TO CELEBRATE THE ENGAGEMENT OF THE MATRIARCHAL NIECE, THEY ARE GATHERING TO CELEBRATE THE LAST BIRTHDAY OF THE PATRIARCH, THEY ARE GATHERING TO WELCOME HOME THE PRODIGAL SON AND HIS BEAUTIFUL GIRLFRIEND AND THEY ARE GOING TO CELEBRATE ALL THIS WITH A SLIDESHOW.

CANDID PHOTOGRAPHS. PHOTOGRAPHS OF THINGS NO ONE THOUGHT ANYONE ELSE KNEW ABOUT. PHOTOGRAPH TAKEN WHEN NO ONE ELSE WAS THERE.

IT'S ALL COMING OUT TODAY. IN BLACK AND WHITE FOR EVERYONE TO SEE. THE REMNANTS OF CHILD ABUSE, INFIDELITY, LOSS, DESTRUCTION AND MISSED BIRTHDAY PARTIES. IT'S ALL COMING OUT. IT'S GOING TO BE A LONG NIGHT. POSSIBLY FOREVER.

The Recruitment Officer

By

Thomas Alexander

Tom, a charming Yankee recruiter, comes to an unspecified English town and falls in love with the conference centre manager, Julia.

But what exactly is he recruiting for? Why does everyone who joins never come back and what is on the other side of the door

Where do the recruits go after signing up?

An existential love story that asks questions of who we are, what we want from life and whether we're getting it, The Recruitment Officer is a remodelling of the 1706 play by George Farquhar. *The Recruiting Officer*

WRITER'S BLOCK

BY

THOMAS ALEXANDER

PAUL BLOCK WAS ONCE A PROLIFIC WRITER. A RECIPIENT OF BOTH THE PEN AND FAULKNER-AWARDS AND THE AUTHOR OF OVER TEN DIFFERENT NOVELS, HE WAS ONCE CONSIDERED THE UK'S MOST UP AND COMING WRITER UNTIL, AT THE AGE OF FORTY, HE SUFFERED A NERVOUS BREAKDOWN.

TEN YEARS LATER THE WORLD HAS FORGOTTEN PAUL BLOCK. HOLED UP IN HIS STUDY HE HAS BEEN WORKING ON THE SAME FIRST PAGE OF HIS NEW NOVEL FOR NEARLY FIVE YEARS, KEPT COMPANY BY ONLY HIS MAID, A FOUL MOUTHED IRISH HIT-MAN, A VETERAN OF THE BATTLE OF GETTYSBURG AND A NINETEEN FORTIES FEMME FETAL.

TODAY, ALL THAT'S GOING TO CHANGE. PAUL HAS A BUSY DAY AHEAD OF HIM. FIRST HE'S GOING TO KILL A PERSISTENT AND CHARMLESS YOUNG REPORTER WHO WANTS TO DO A PIECE ON 'WRITER'S BLOCK' AND THEN HE'S GOING TO HAVE A RARE VISIT FROM HIS SON WHO'S BRINGING HIM BAD NEWS AND A NEW COUCH.

WITH A MISSING BODY AND A SON WHO HATES HIM, PAUL MUST FINALLY RID HIMSELF OF HIS PROTAGONISTS IF HE'S EVER GOING TO STAY OUT OF JAIL, AND FINISH THAT FIRST PAGE.

Writing William
By
Thomas Alexander

"We want to put our education to use and our education is, was, and god damned always will be William fucking Shakespeare! We want lines we don't understand. We want plot holes so big you can drive a truck through them! We want to make sense of it all! Or at least understand what we studied it for in the first place! You want to put on a play? We want Shakespeare!"

Released in commemoration of Shakespeare's 450th anniversary this special edition of Writing William contains the original playbill and deleted scenes along with a new forward by Thomas Alexander.

Writing William follows a young, aspiring, playwright who, in order to get his work on stage, forges a Shakespeare play.

Basing the play on the relationship between Henry II and Eleanor of Aquitaine during the murder of Thomas Becket, Will, starts to see it mirror his own failing marriage as he struggles to find approval from an unforgiving spouse.

Backed by a working class billionaire and supported by an array of aging actors, the lead of which is mute, Will finds cathartic release in the writing of the play and it's impending production, but he hasn't taken into account just how gullible the theatre going public truly are.

COMMEMORATIVE 450TH BIRTHDAY EDITION

A PLAY ABOUT LOVE, THEATRE & PLAGIARISM

Writing William

By

Thomas Alexander
Shakespeare

INCLUDES FORWARD BY AUTHOR
DELETED SCENES & ORIGINAL PLAYBILL

cover design by SimplyA:

A comedic farce, Writing William blends Shakespearian dialogue with modern humour and innovative staging to look at the relationship of the artist and his art, the burden of success upon a relationship, and the true cost of producing a play.

THOMAS

Japan, 1945 – A Family At War

When a wandering priest escaping a troubled past is taken in by a prominent family, a quiet city in northern Japan is forced to confront the dark shadows of war seeping into their lives in ways they could never have anticipated.

With its townsmen scattered throughout the farthest ends of a desperate empire in a final defence against the encroaching West, the idyllic northern city of Morioka, far removed from the harsh realities of the front, is largely left to itself.

THOMAS ALEXANDER

A Scattering of Orphans

But when a prominent doctor is conscripted and sent to Manila, his sister is left as head of the household and must deal with a young priest living at the bottom of their garden with a large collection of maps and strange knowledge of English.

As the cold hand of war approaches, each person must choose their own destiny and place in the new world.

THE OTHER SIDE

ALEXANDER

Commemorating the 70th Anniversary of the end of WW2! A trilogy spanning the length of the war from the viewpoint of an ordinary Japanese family.

Thomas Alexander

The Disingenuous Martyr

omas Alexander

Beyond The Noonday Sun

Offering a unique perspective through the eyes of a rural Japanese family into the impact of history's bloodiest war to date, *A Scattering of Orphans* is one family's attempt to make sense of a changing world amidst the desolation of war, both home and abroad.

DIRECT LIGHT

OF THE SUN

DIRECT
LIGHT